AF413642

General Gabe and the Big Fish

Christine Hebert, Ph.D.

DEDICATED TO MY THREE
GRANDCHILDREN
CALEN
MILA
& ISABELLA

This is the true story of
General Gabriel Maupin
My 8th great grandfather
He is buried at
Bruton Parish
In
Williamsburg, Virginia

Records of this event are stored
in the
Virginia State Archives.

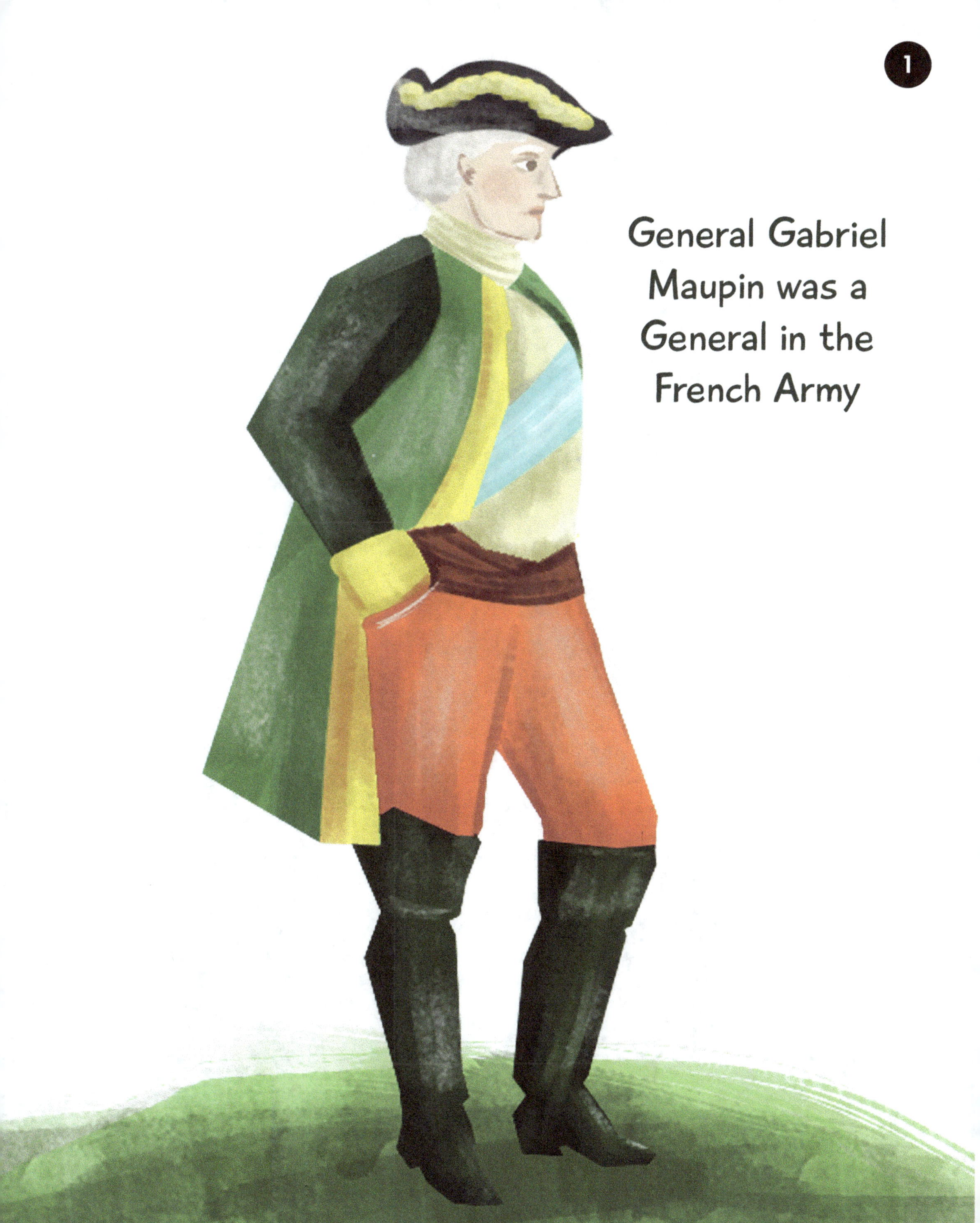
General Gabriel
Maupin was a
General in the
French Army

Gabe was a very religious Christian. He loved God.

General Gabe did not worship
God the same way the King
Charles did. The King wanted
everyone to worship like he did.

The King decided that everyone who did not worship God the way he did had to leave the country in 30 days.

The kind General and his family had to leave their land and most belongings behind and leave the country. They were sad.

His family took a ship to Ireland in the 1690's and then in 1700 they took a ship to Virginia to start a new life where they could worship as they pleased.

The General had a nice cabin on the ship. He read, studied, and prayed there. He became a leader on the ship, leading prayers and studies. The trip would take 3 months.

One day, a few days before they were to arrive in Yorktown, Virginia, the boat developed a leak.

The crew worked very hard to pump
the water out of the ship.

The water came in faster than they could pump it out and it seemed as though the ship would sink.

Some of the crew and passengers
knocked on General Gabe's cabin door.

They knew he loved God. They begged him to pray for the ship saying, "Pray for us lest we perish."

General Gabe immediately began to pray and asked God for the ship to be spared.

Suddenly, the leak stopped!

The crew was able to pump
the water out and they
could finish their journey.

The passengers and crew rejoiced.

When they arrived in Virginia, they told everyone about the miracle they experienced and the power of prayer.

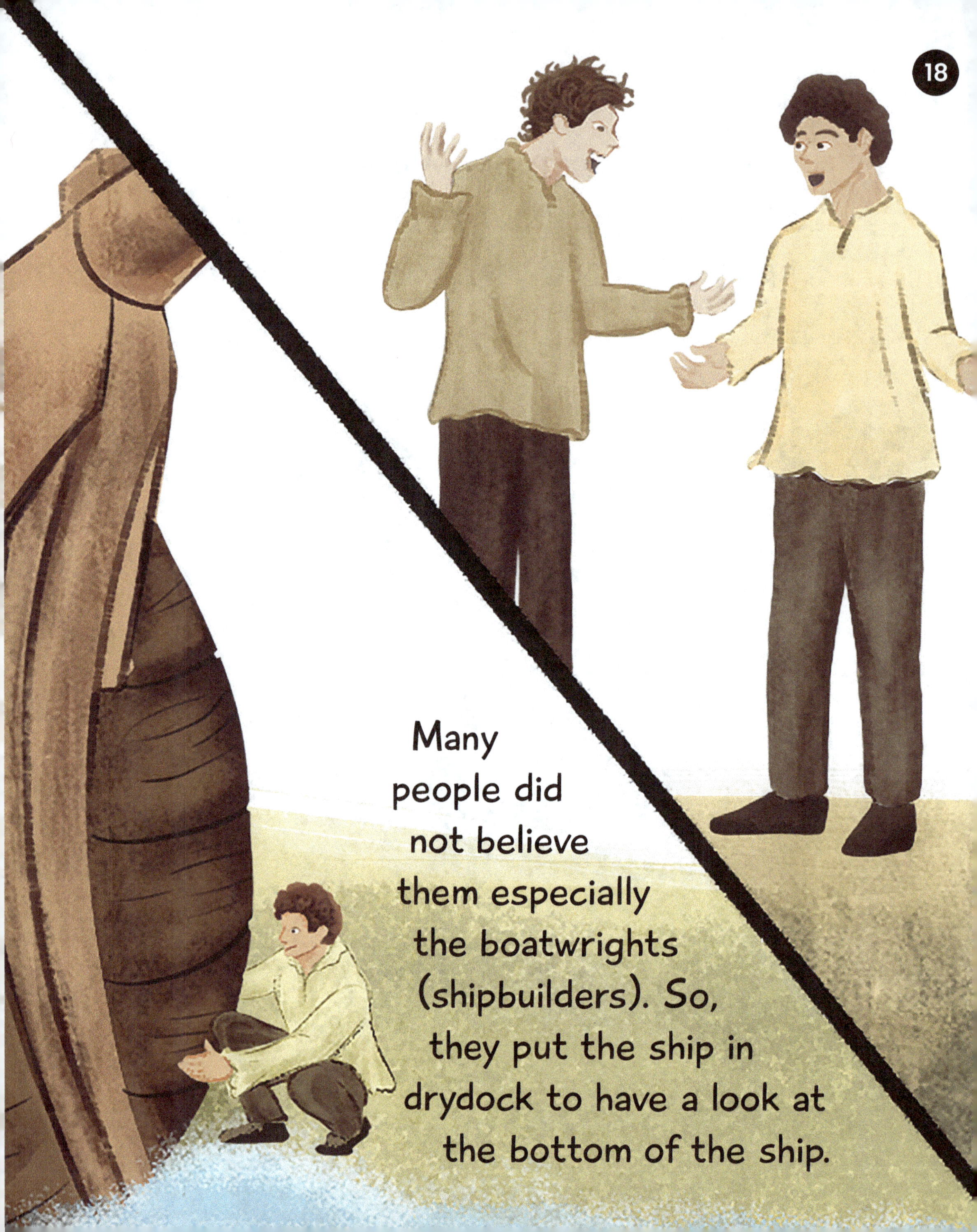

Many people did not believe them especially the boatwrights (shipbuilders). So, they put the ship in drydock to have a look at the bottom of the ship.

19
There they found a big fish had become stuck in the hole in the ship and had stopped the leak.

After his arrival, the General started
a tavern and restaurant in Williamsburg
which is now the Williamsburg Inn.

Always believe in God's power
and the power of prayer.

THE END